THE POWER

of

DIVINE INTERVENTION

And it shall come to pass, that before they call, I will answer; and while they are yet speaking, I will hear.

Isaiah 65:24

by

Franklin N. Abazie

The power of divine intervention
COPYRIGHT 2020 BY Franklin N Abazie
ISBN: 978:1-945-133-68-8

All right reserved. This book or any portion thereof may not be reproduced or used in any manner whatsoever without the express written permission of the publisher, except for the use of brief quotations in a book review. All Bible quotes are from King James Version and others as noted.

Published by:
F N ABAZIE PUBLISHING HOUSE---a.k.a,
EMPOWERMENT BOOKSTORE:

That I may publish with the voice of thanksgiving and tell of all thy wondrous works.
Psalms26:7

To order additional copies, wholesales or booking:
Call the Church office (973-372-7518)
or Empowerment Bookstore Hotline 973-393-8518

Worship address:
343 Sanford Avenue Newark New Jersey 07106
Administrative Head Office address:
33 Schley Street Newark New Jersey 07112
Email:pastorfranknto@yahoo.com
Website www.fnabaziehealingministries.org
Publishing House: www.fnabaziepublishinghouse.org

This book is a production of F N Abazie
Publishing House. A publication Arms of
Miracle of God Ministries 2020
First Edition

CONTENTS

The Mandate of The Commission iv

Arms of The Commission v

Introduction ix

CHAPTER 1 42
The Secret of Answered Prayer

CHAPTER 2 63
Acess Keys to Provoke Divine Intervention

CHAPTER 3 118
Prayer of Salvation

CHAPTER 4 128
About The Author

Books by Rev Franklin N Abazie 131

The Power of Divine Intervention

THE MANDATE OF THE COMMISSION

"THE MOMENT IS DUE TO IMPACT YOUR WORLD THROUGH THE REVIVAL OF THE HEALING & MIRACLE MINISTRY OF JESUS CHRIST OF NAZARETH."

"I AM SENDING YOU TO RESTORE HEALTH UNTO THEE AND I WILL HEAL THEE OF THY WOUNDS, SAID THE LORD OF HOST."

ARMS OF THE COMMISSION

1) F N Abazie Ministries-Miracle of God Ministries (Miracle Chapel Intl)
2) F N Abazie TV Ministries: Global Television Ministry Outreach.
3) F N Abazie Radio Ministries: Radio Broadcasting Outreach.
4) F N Abazie Publishing House: Book Publication.
5) F N Abazie Bible School: also called Word of Healing Bible School (W.O.H.B.S)
6) F N Abazie Evangelistic Ass: Miracle of God Ministries: Global Crusade
7) Empowerment Bookstore: Book distribution.
8) F N Abazie Helping Hands: Meeting the help of the needy world wide
9) F N Abazie Disaster Recovery Mission: Global Disaster Recovery.
10) F N Abazie Prison Ministry: Prison Ministry for all convicts "Second chance"

Some of our ministry arms are waiting the appointed time to commence.

FAVOR CONFESSION

Father thank you for making me righteous and accepted through the blood of Jesus Christ. Because of that, I am blessed and highly favored by God. I am the subject of your affection. Your favor surrounds me as a shield, and the first thing that people see around me is your favored shield.

Thank you that I have favor with you and man today. All day long people go out of their way to bless me and help me. I have favor with everyone that I deal with today. Doors that were once closed are now opened for me. I receive preferential treatment, and I have special privileges, I am Gods favored child.

No good thing will he withhold from me. Because of Gods favor my enemies cannot triumph over my life. I have supernatural increase and promotion. I declare restoration to everything that the devil has stolen from my life. I have honor in the midst of my adversaries and an increase in assets, especially in real estate and expansion of territories.

Because I am highly favored by God, I experience great victories, supernatural turnarounds, and miraculous breakthrough in the midst of great impossibilities. I receive recognition, prominence, and honor. Petitions are granted to me even by ungodly authorities. Policies, rules, regulations, and laws are changed and reverse on my behalf.

I win battles that I don't even have to fight, because God fights them for me. This is the day, the set time and the designated moment for me to experience the free favor of God, that profusely and lavishly abound on my behalf in Jesus name. **Amen.**

INTRODUCTION

"And it shall come to pass, that before they call, I will answer; and while they are yet speaking, I will hear." **Isaiah 65:24**

I may never get the chance to meet with you, but I am happy you picked *up courage to* read this book: ***"THE POWER OF DIVINE INTERVENTION".*** Divine intervention is the sudden move of God upon a man's situation.

Divine intervention is the help of God in time of need. In other words, divine intervention is the acts of God that we all call a miracle. Divine intervention is when God uses His power to overcome a helpless situation. The Gospel of Jesus is the Gospel of power.

"For I am not ashamed of the gospel of Christ: for it is the power of God unto

Introduction

salvation to everyone that believeth; to the Jew first, and also to the Greek."
Romans1:16

It is my joy to encourage you to have a prayer lifestyle. It is also my joy to encourage you to pray without ceasing. In acts chapter 12, although Herod the king was the physical ruler, it was the church that ruled spiritually by prayer. (See acts 12:1-10)

"Peter therefore was kept in prison: but prayer was made without ceasing of the church unto God for him." **Acts12:5**

Anyone can access the power of divine intervention through continual prayer and supplication.

"But we will give ourselves continually to prayer, and to the ministry of the word."
Acts6:4

If you can pray without ceasing, plus continual praise in your mouth, then you will be unstoppable before every devil. "I will bless the Lord at all times: his praise shall continually be in my mouth." **Psalm34:1**

"And this is the confidence that we have in him that, if we ask any thing according to his will, he heareth us: **1John5:14**

However, to provoke divine intervention, we must pray according to *"His will"*

Jesus taught us to pray in Luke 11:2-4

"And he said unto them, When ye pray, say, Our Father which art in heaven, Hallowed be thy name. Thy kingdom come. Thy will be done, as in heaven, so in earth. Give us day by day our daily bread. And forgive us our sins; for we also forgive every one that is indebted to us. And lead us not into temptation; but deliver us from evil." Luke11:2-4

Introduction

The Holy Bible clearly states that whatever we ask, we know that we have the petitions that we desired of him. *And if we know that he hear us, whatsoever we ask, we know that we have the petitions that we desired of him."* **1John 5:15**

It took the power of divine intervention to release Peter from prison.

"And, behold, the angel of the Lord came upon him, and a light shined in the prison: and he smote Peter on the side, and raised him up, saying, Arise up quickly. And his chains fell off from his hands."

And the angel said unto him, Gird thyself, and bind on thy sandals. And so he did. And he saith unto him, Cast thy garment about thee, and follow me." **See Acts 12:7-8**

It took divine intervention to release Daniel from the lion's den unhurt.

The Power of Divine Intervention

"My God hath sent his angel, and hath shut the lions' mouths, that they have not hurt me: forasmuch as before him innocency was found in me; and also before thee, O king, have I done no hurt." Daniel 6:22

It took the power of divine intervention to protect Shadrach Meshach and Abednego from the fury furnace of the fire.

"Then Nebuchadnezzar spake, and said, Blessed be the God of Shadrach, Meshach, and Abednego, who hath sent his angel, and delivered his servants that trusted in him, and have changed the king's word, and yielded their bodies, that they might not serve nor worship any god, except their own God." **Daniel3:28**

It took the Power of divine intervention for Peter to walk on the water.

Introduction

"And Peter answered him and said, Lord, if it be thou, bid me come unto thee on the water."

"And he said, Come. And when Peter was come down out of the ship, he walked on the water, to go to Jesus."

See Mathew14:28-29

It took the power of divine intervention for the children of Isreal to cross through the red sea.

It took divine intervention to feed five thousand men besides women and children.

"And he commanded the multitude to sit down on the grass, and took the five loaves, and the two fishes, and looking up to heaven, he blessed, and brake, and gave the loaves to his disciples, and the disciples to the multitude.

And they did all eat, and were filled: and they took up of the fragments that remained twelve baskets full.

And they that had eaten were about five thousand men, beside women and children."

See Mathew14:19-21

I pray may God grant you divine intervention as you pray. May God visit your life and change your story in Jesus mighty Name. **Amen**

Come with me let's examine what the Holy Spirit is saying in this book.

HIS DESTINY WAS THE CROSS....

HIS PURPOSE WAS LOVE....

HIS REASON WAS YOU....

"Whoever loves discipline loves knowledge, but he who hates reproof is stupid."

Proverbs12:1

As many as I love, I rebuke and chasten: be zealous therefore, and repent.

Rev 3:19

"I therefore so run, not as uncertainly; so fight I, not as one that beateth the air:"

1cor9:26

"But I keep under my body, and bring it into subjection: lest that by any means, when I have preached to others, I myself should be a castaway."

1cor9:27

"I must work the works of him that sent me, while it is day: the night cometh, when no man can work."

John9:4

"Whoever spares the rod hates his son, but he who loves him is diligent to discipline him."

Proverbs13:24

"Those whom I love, I reprove and discipline, so be zealous and repent."

Revelation 3:19

"The rod and reproof give wisdom, but a child left to himself brings shame to his mother."

Proverbs 29:15

"So he fed them according to the integrity of his heart; and guided them by the skilfulness of his hands."

Psalm 78:72

"And ye have forgotten the exhortation which speaketh unto you as unto children, My son, despise not thou the chastening of the Lord, nor faint when thou art rebuked of him:"

Hebrews 12:5

"For whom the Lord loveth he chasteneth, and scourgeth every son whom he receiveth."

Hebrews12:6

"If ye endure chastening, God dealeth with you as with sons; for what son is he whom the father chasteneth not"?

Hebrews 12:7

"But if ye be without chastisement, whereof all are partakers, then are ye bastards, and not sons."

Hebrews 12:8

"Furthermore we have had fathers of our flesh which corrected us, and we gave them reverence: shall we not much rather be in subjection unto the Father of spirits, and live?"

Hebrews12:9

"He that spareth his rod hateth his son: but he that loveth him chasteneth him betimes."

Proverbs 13:24

xxx

"Let thy work appear unto thy servants, and thy glory unto their children."

Psalm 90:16

"And let the beauty of the Lord our God be upon us: and establish thou the work of our hands upon us; yea, the work of our hands establish thou it."

Psalm90:17

"And he shall be like a tree planted by the rivers of water, that bringeth forth his fruit in his season; his leaf also shall not wither; and whatsoever he doeth shall prosper."

Psalm1:3

"I must work the works of him that sent me, while it is day: the night cometh, when no man can work."

John9:4

"For even when we were with you, this we commanded you, that if any would not work, neither should he eat."

2theo3:10

"And that ye study to be quiet, and to do your own business, and to work with your own hands, as we commanded you;

1theo4:11

"To discipline a child produces wisdom, but a mother is disgraced by an undisciplined child."

Proverbs 29:15

"Whoever loves discipline loves knowledge, but whoever hates correction is stupid."

Proverbs 12:1

"Blessed is the one whom God corrects; so do not despise the discipline of the Almighty."

Job 5:17

"Blessed is the one you discipline, LORD, the one you teach from your law;"

Psalm 94:12

But Jesus answered them, My Father worketh hitherto, and I work.
John5:17

CHAPTER 1

THE SECRET OF ANSWERED PRAYER

"Call unto me, and I will answer thee, and show thee great and mighty things, which thou knowest not."
Jeremiah33:3

The *Power of Divine intervention*, loosely defined is- *God intervening in the affairs of man. "If there is a man to pray, there is a God to answer."* Let me say this, until God takes over a particular circumstance, there is still hope. *For there is hope of a tree, if it be cut down, that it will sprout again, and that the tender branch thereof will not cease.*

My bible says...

Chapter 1 : The Secret of Answered Prayer

"For to him that is joined to all the living there is hope: for a living dog is better than a dead lion". **Eccl9:4**

We were told……

"Call unto me, and I will answer thee, and show thee great and mighty things, which thou knowest not." **Jer33:3**

"And it shall come to pass, that before they call, I will answer; and while they are yet speaking, I will hear." **Isaiah65:24**

"Seek ye the Lord while he may be found, call ye upon him while he is near." **Isaiah55:6**

Divine intervention is the result of answered prayers. Although the atheists, agnostics, and deists may have a different explanations to it, but for believers who are *grounded in the faith*, we see God in everything that we do. *Divine intervention* is clearly the finger of God in the life of a man.

The Power of Divine Intervention

"And it shall come to pass, that before they call, I will answer; and while they are yet speaking, I will hear." **Isaiah65:24**

"Seek ye the Lord while he may be found, call ye upon him while he is near. **Isaiah55:6**

Divine intervention is the manifestation of the Spirit of God upon our life.

I urge you to attribute anything that happened in your life, every turn of events, or the outcome of some of the most prevailing circumstances in your life to God.

Hear this….Answered prayer simply mean *divine intervention.*

"Then said he unto me, Fear not, Daniel: for from the first day that thou didst set thine heart to understand, and to chasten thyself before thy God, thy words were heard, and I am come for thy words." **Daniel10:12**

Chapter 1 : The Secret of Answered Prayer

What is Divine Intervention?

Have you ever heard when people say... this will take God?

Divine intervention is the sudden movement of God upon your life. *Divine intervention is when God turns around the outcome of your prevailing situation. Divine intervention is when God favors a man in the midst of unpredicted circumstance.* Divine intervention is simply the favor of God upon the life of a man. Permit me to prophesy victory and prosperity over your life in the Name of Jesus. Amen

Divine intervention is the move of God that proves the sovereignty and supremacy of the acts of God.

It is When God supernaturally intervenes into a situation, when all hopes have been lost.

The Power of Divine Intervention

Talking about Lazarus in John chapter 11

"Jesus said, Take ye away the stone. Martha, the sister of him that was dead, saith unto him, Lord, by this time he stinketh: for he hath been dead four days. Jesus saith unto her, Said I not unto thee, that, if thou wouldest believe, thou shouldest see the glory of God?"

John11:39-40

When Do You Need Divine Intervention?

As believers, we must believe and trust in God. We must also look up to God for help in times of trouble.

"I will lift up mine eyes unto the hills, from whence cometh my help. My help cometh from the Lord, which made heaven and earth. He will not suffer thy foot to

Chapter 1 : The Secret of Answered Prayer

be moved: he that keepeth thee will not slumber. Behold, he that keepeth Israel shall neither slumber nor sleep.

The Lord is thy keeper: the Lord is thy shade upon thy right hand. The sun shall not smite thee by day, nor the moon by night. The Lord shall preserve thee from all evil: he shall preserve thy soul. The Lord shall preserve thy going out and thy coming in from this time forth, and even for evermore." **Psalms121:1-8**

Israel was in bondage in Egypt

If God did not step in, there would have been no deliverance. Pharaoh was just too strong for the entire nation of Israel.

David found himself in miry clay; the more he struggled to be free, the deeper he sank. If God did not step in, there would be no escape.

Lazarus was already dead.

It took the authority of the Lord Jesus to bring Lazarus to life.

The Poor Widow

In 2 Kings 4, a poor widow owed so much money, the creditors came to take her two sons in lieu of the money owed. If God did not intervene, there could be no hope anywhere.

Simon Peter

In Acts 12, Simon Peter was locked up in prison, awaiting to be be-headed by Herod, like he did with James. If God did not intervene, Peter's untimely demise would have been history.

These cases were real scenarios in the Scriptures. Nevertheless, God stepped in and there was a complete turnaround..

Chapter 1 : The Secret of Answered Prayer

What is your own situation that you want God to take over? A bondage? A miry clay? A debt? A prison? A sickness? A seemingly endless family crisis? Or what?

If God intervened in those days, He will intervene today. *Jesus Christ is the same yesterday, today and forever.*

Call upon the Lord with all your heart. Report that situation to Him. *Ask Him to do something spectacular*. Tell Him exactly what you want. Believe Him with all your heart. He will deliver you and you shall glorify Him.

God loves to intervene in seemingly impossible situations, if He is invited in. Invite Him today and He will surprise you.

HOW DOES GOD INTERVENE?

God responds to the cry of His people.

Hear this… God has power to do as He pleases. It is God's will to do as he pleases.

No one can impose themselves on God. If it's God's will, God will intervene, if not God will do nothing. *"Whatsoever the Lord pleased, that did he in heaven, and in earth, in the seas, and all deep places".*

Often some of us get angry when they needed God to for example revive their cancer sick uncle. Yet God took them Home. God is Omnipotent, He will do as he pleases. *"But our God is in the heavens: he hath done whatsoever he hath pleased."* **Psalm115:3**

Irrespective of your position, and regardless of your statue, or faith in God, God will do according to His Divine Will.

"According as his divine power hath given unto us all things that pertain unto life and godliness, through the knowledge of him that hath called us to glory and virtue: Whereby are given unto us exceeding great and precious promises: that by these ye

Chapter 1 : The Secret of Answered Prayer

might be partakers of the divine nature, having escaped the corruption that is in the world through lust."

"For whom he did foreknow, he also did predestinate to be conformed to the image of his Son, that he might be the firstborn among many brethren. Moreover whom he did predestinate, them he also called: and whom he called, them he also justified: and whom he justified, them he also glorified."

When Do We Need Divine Intervention?

------- *When we are in a dead-end job*--------

The truth is-*there some dead end jobs that will take only the power of divine intervention for you to come out of it*. I pray for you if you are in such a situation I pronounce your emancipation and freedom now in the Name of Jesus Christ of Nazareth. I ask God to have mercy. I ask

God to forgive you and make away for you now in Jesus Name. *Behold, I will do a new thing; now it shall spring forth; shall ye not know it? I will even make a way in the wilderness, and rivers in the desert*

-- When there is no human solution to your problem--

I have seen *cancer terminal patients* written off *by doctors* to go *home* and *die in peace.* "…for he hath said, I will never leave thee, nor forsake thee." In my opinion *"only God have the final say".*

Your case is not over until Gods takes over. *When my father and my mother forsake me, then the Lord will take me up. Teach me thy way, O Lord, and lead me in a plain path, because of mine enemies.* Even when men have given up on you, I want you to believe God for divine intervention. *Behold, I am the Lord, the God of all flesh: is there any thing too hard for me?*

Chapter 1 : The Secret of Answered Prayer

------*When people ask you Where is your God?*--------

There are season in your life that God must show himself strong on your behalf. There comes a time when all hope is lost, that only the *power of divine intervention* will redeem the case.

"And Elijah came unto all the people, and said, How long halt ye between two opinions? if the Lord be God, follow him: but if Baal, then follow him. And the people answered him not a word." **1King18:21**

Here this……

Divine intervention will silent all your mockers. "And call ye on the name of your gods, and I will call on the name of the Lord: and the God that answereth by fire, let him be God. And all the people answered and said, It is well spoken." **1king18:24**

−−*When you are not making progress in life*−−

It is God's will for everyone to experience progressive prosperity. *If you have not been making progress in your life, you are a candidate of divine intervention.* The *power of divine intervention* will change your life. *But the path of the just is as the shining light, that shineth more and more unto the perfect day.*

KEYS TO EXPERIENCE DIVINE INTERVENTION

---------------*Be Humble*-------------

Humility is a principle of the kingdom of God. *It is a law,* if you humble yourself, God will exalt you in due time. *He hath put down the mighty from their seats, and exalted them of low degree. We were told....*

Humility is the *key to experience God*. Humility is the platform for the manifestation *divine power*. Humble

Chapter 1 : The Secret of Answered Prayer

yourselves therefore under the mighty hand of God, that he may exalt you in due time: If you are proud God will not give you more grace. *But he giveth more grace. Wherefore he saith, God resisteth the proud, but giveth grace unto the humble.*

-----*Come to God with expectations*-----

For unless you expect something to happen. God will not do anything. *God looks for your expectation. If you want to see anything then, expect it to happen.* (See Acts 3:5; Proverbs 23:18; Psalm 62:5)

------------*Come with praise*------------

We were told God dwells in praise. *"But thou art holy, O thou that inhabitest the praises of Israel."* God will only manifest His power upon those who can praise Him. Remember….. He does not share His Glory. *"I am the Lord: that is my name: and my glory will I not give to another, neither my praise to graven images."* **Isaiah 42:8**

The Power of Divine Intervention

-----*Come in the Name of Jesus Christ*-----

The Name of Jesus is wonderful and Powerful. The Name of Jesus is the Power of attorney for every other name to bow to. The access code to answered prayers is the Name of Jesus. *"And whatsoever ye shall ask in my name, that will I do, that the Father may be glorified in the Son. If ye shall ask any thing in my name, I will do it."* Access into the supernatural and to experience divine intervention is the Name of Jesus. *In my name shall they cast out devils; they shall speak with new tongues;* If you want to see miracles in your life, embrace and call the Name of Jesus in your prayers and every time you are in need.

----*Believe in the Name of Jesus Christ*----

You shall be blessed if you believe in the Name of Jesus Christ. The word says *"And blessed is she that believed: for there shall*

Chapter 1 : The Secret of Answered Prayer

be a performance of those things which were told her from the Lord." **Luke1:45**

------------*Come with trust*--------------

God is looking for trust. *If you cannot trust God, how can he manifest His power upon your life?* "They that trust in the Lord shall be as mount Zion, which cannot be removed, but abideth for ever. As the mountains are round about Jerusalem, so the Lord is round about his people from henceforth even forever." **Psalm125:1-2**

--------- *Come crying for mercy*---------

God is looking for a contrite heart. *The sacrifices of God are a broken spirit: a broken and a contrite heart, O God, thou wilt not despise.* It is only the mercy of God that will open our heavens for us. If you must experience open heaven you must come to God with a contrite heart. Some of us do not understand; it is only the mercy of God that will destroy anything hindering our prayer. "By mercy and truth iniquity is purged: and by the fear of the Lord men depart from evil." **Proverb 16:6**

"So then it is not of him that willeth, nor of him that runneth, but of God that sheweth mercy." **Romans 9:16**

"When I cry unto thee, then shall mine enemies turn back: this I know; for God is for me." **Psalm 56:9**

WHAT ARE WE SAYING?

For anyone to see *God's Power*, they must be able to pray all the time. Spiritual people are righteous men and women who know how to connect to God. *God will always do as He pleases.* There is *power in divine intervention*. If you are a praying man or woman like me, I encourage you to keep praying. Do not faint for in due time you shall reap.

Chapter 1 : The Secret of Answered Prayer

THE BENEFITS OF DIVINE INTERVENTION

-----It converts unbelievers-----

Unbelievers will not accept the Lord Jesus unless they see a sign. *"And brought them out, and said, Sirs, what must I do to be saved? And they said, Believe on the Lord Jesus Christ, and thou shalt be saved, and thy house."*

And it shall come to pass, if they will not believe thee, neither hearken to the voice of the first sign, that they will believe the voice of the latter sign.

--------------It brings Joy---------------

And the people with one accord gave heed unto those things which Philip spake, hearing and seeing the miracles which he did……..And there was great joy in that city.

The miracles of God are the source of joy in our lives. No one will witness *a miracle* and not be happy.

BELIEVE GOD FOR SUPERNATURAL FAVOR.

Miracles are deliberate act of God, provoke by the desperate faith in men.

There is supernatural power in the things we say daily. I commend you to rise up and speak up. You must take advantage of your future by speak the right word.

The power of the spoken word is a concept shared by many cultures and its roots go deep into pre-literate history. The most widely cited written reference in western civilization comes from the Bible.

Chapter 1 : The Secret of Answered Prayer

YOU ARE IN SPIRITUAL CAPTIVITY BY THE WAY YOU THINK

Although our thoughts are powerful, the spoken word is even more powerful. We must change the way we think, especially before we speak out any word. *"Thou art snared with the words of thy mouth, thou art taken with the words of thy mouth." Proverb6:2*

"For as he thinketh in his heart, so is he: Eat and drink, saith he to thee; but his heart is not with thee." **Proverb23:7**

"A good man out of the good treasure of his heart bringeth forth that which is good; and an evil man out of the evil treasure of his heart bringeth forth that which is evil: for of the abundance of the heart his mouth speaketh" **Luke6:45**

CHAPTER 2
ACESS KEYS TO PROVOKE DIVINE INTERVENTION

"Peter therefore was kept in prison: but prayer was made without ceasing of the church unto God for him."
Acts12:5

The above scripture simply explains to us that, for anyone to provoke divine intervention, *prayer must be made without ceasing.* In the above scriptural passage in acts chapter twelve from verse one, although King Herold was the physical authority, the church ruled via prayers.

The most powerful people on earth are *intercessors.* The people that prays without ceasing in faith always dominate

Chapter 2: Acess Keys to Provoke Divine Intervention

the challenges that come their way in life. *One time the queen of England said, I fear nothing but the prayers of John Knox.*

John Knox from Scotland was a powerful man of prayer in the last century. *If you desire continual access onto the supernatural you must have a consistent prayer lifestyle.* In Mark Chapter six, the King was afraid of John the Baptist-the preacher.

"For Herod feared John, knowing that he was a just man and an holy, and observed him; and when he heard him, he did many things, and heard him gladly." **Mark 6:20**

Access keys to provoke divine intervention

---------------- *Be humble*-----------------

Whenever you stay humbled in life, people do not expect much from you. *We were told that pride goeth before a fall.* As long as you are humble you will always have access to activate divine intervention continually.

---------------Be meek---------------

I will encourage you to always take life easy. Never put pressure on your-self. *Jesus said "Come unto me, all ye that labour and are heavy laden, and I will give you rest. Take my yoke upon you, and learn of me; for I am meek and lowly in heart: and ye shall find rest unto your souls. For my yoke is easy, and my burden is light."* **Mathew 11:28-30**

As long as you are meek you will inherit the earth. Moses because of meekness became the greatest of all times among the prophets. *Now the man Moses was very meek, above all the men which [were] upon the face of the earth.* **Number 12:3**

Without the spirit of meekness you will not be able to accomplish your assignment.

Jesus because of meekness accomplished his task here on earth. **"And being found in fashion as a man, he humbled himself, and became obedient unto death, even the death of the cross." Phil2:8**

You will always have access to the riches of the earth. Remember, "The earth is the Lord's, and the fulness thereof; the world, and they that dwell therein.

"Blessed are the meek: for they shall inherit the earth." **Mathew5:5**

"The earth is the Lord's, and the fulness thereof; the world, and they that dwell therein." **Psalm24:1**

"To speak evil of no man, to be no brawlers, [but] gentle, shewing all meekness unto all men." **Titus 3:2**

"But the meek shall inherit the earth; and shall delight themselves in the abundance of peace." **Psalms 37:11**

"The meek will he guide in judgment: and the meek will he teach his way." **Psalms 25:9**

"Who [is] a wise man and endued with knowledge among you? let him shew out of a good conversation his works with meekness of wisdom." **James 3:13**

"But [let it be] the hidden man of the heart, in that which is not corruptible, [even the ornament] of a meek and quiet spirit, which is in the sight of God of great price." **1 Peter 3:4 -**

"But sanctify the Lord God in your hearts: and [be] ready always to [give] an answer to every man that asketh you a reason of the hope that is in you with meekness and fear:" **1 Peter 3:15**

(Now the man Moses was very meek, above all the men which [were] upon the face of the earth.) **Numbers 12:3 -**

Chapter 2: Acess Keys to Provoke Divine Intervention

"But the fruit of the Spirit is love, joy, peace, longsuffering, gentleness, goodness, faith." **Galatians 5:22**

-------------*Be prayerful*--------------------

Without a prayer lifestyle you cannot provoke divine intervention. Prayer is the superior access key, that work with faith to provoke the supernatural. The bible says ... ***And the prayer of faith shall save the sick,* and the Lord shall raise him up; and if he have committed sins, they shall be forgiven him**.

The position of *prayers to provoke divine intervention* is unquestionable. Without prayer we have no access. Prayer is our only communication channel to speak to God.

Prayer is the channel to pour out our heart desire, vent our anger, and confess our sins. My bible says *"Confess your faults one to another, and pray one for another, that ye may be healed. The effectual fervent prayer of a righteous man availeth much."* **James 5:16**

John the revelator puts it this way—*"If we confess our sins, he is faithful and just to forgive us our sins, and to cleanse us from all unrighteousness."* **1John1:9**

What am I saying?

If you know how to pray and praise continually, you will never lack breakthrough in life. David said…. I will bless the Lord at all times: his praise shall continually be in my mouth.

A Prayer lifestyle and continual praise is an access key into unlimited breakthroughs in the life of the believer. Whenever your joy is depleted, you will be short changed of testimony. *"The vine is dried up, and the fig tree languisheth; the pomegranate tree, the palm tree also, and the apple tree, even all the trees of the field, are withered: because joy is withered away from the sons of men."* **Joel 1:12**

I will encourage you to always maintain a life full of joy if you must continue to enjoy breakthroughs in life. The bible puts it this way in Isaiah chapter twelve verse three *Therefore with joy shall ye draw water out of the wells of salvation.*

Please note, another word for salvation in the above scripture is the word deliverance. So it's literally saying therefore with joy shall ye draw water out of the well of deliverance.

MANIFESTATION OF THE SUPERNATURAL

"And Jesus took the loaves; and when he had given thanks, he distributed to the disciples, and the disciples to them that were

set down; and likewise of the fishes as much as they would." **John 6:11**

Although it may seem like the supernatural is exclusively for those in the kingdom. The truth is, it is for all of us. Often we steal the glory of God by not sharing testimonies of what God has done. We cannot shy away from what God has been doing. If I am permitted to put it this way, *the manifestation of the supernatural is simply testimonies.*

God does whatever that pleases Him. *The Lord thy God in the midst of thee is mighty; he will save, he will rejoice over thee with joy; he will rest in his love, he will joy over thee with singing.*

Faith in God is the key for the *manifestation of the supernatural.* Faith means putting your trust in God. For anyone to understand the "manifestation of faith" (1 Cor. 12:9), we must understand what" faith

Chapter 2: Acess Keys to Provoke Divine Intervention

"Faith" means. Faith is the translation of the Greek noun pistis, which means "trust," "confidence," or "assurance." Our English word "trust" captures the sense very well.

Sadly, most Christians do not know what "faith" is because the modern definition differs from the bible"faith", and the definition most Christians have in their mind, is a "firm belief in something for which there is no proof" (Merriam-Webster's Collegiate Dictionary).

It is vital to understand that "belief in something for which there is no proof" is actually superstition, and that is far from the biblical definition of "faith".

The biblical definition of faith is *"trust,"* and we trust things only after they have been proven to us. God does not ask us to believe Him without some kind of reason or proof. He has left many evidences that He exists and that His Word is true. When God asks us to have faith, He is not asking us to believe something without proof.

All of us have "faith" (trust) in a large number of things. In fact, life would be impossible without trust. A person would not even sit down if he did not trust the chair would hold him. God asks us to trust that Jesus has been raised from the dead because the Bible, history, and evidences such as speaking in tongues, give plenty of evidence for it.

The reason it is impossible to please God without faith (Heb. 11:6), is that after all God does for us day after day, and has done for mankind throughout history, if we still do not trust Him—well you can see that He would be displeased. Frankly, if any of us did many wonderful things for someone else, and that person "returned the favor" by being distrustful of us, we would be displeased too. Once we understand that "faith" is "trust", we are in a position

Chapter 2: Acess Keys to Provoke Divine Intervention

to understand the "manifestation of faith," which we might also call, "the manifestation of trust."

In contrast to ordinary faith, the manifestation of Holy Spirit referred to as "faith" is the trust that is necessary to accomplish the special tasks that God, by revelation, asks us to do. Contrasting "faith" with the "manifestation of faith" should help to clarify what that means. If I own a chair that I have sat in many times, I have built up trust that it will hold me. I have faith in the chair.

But what about doing a healing or miracle? I know I cannot do it in my flesh. Therefore, the only way I can heal or do a miracle is to trust in the revelation that I have received from God (via a message of knowledge, wisdom, or discerning of spirit), and to trust that when I command the healing or miracle to come to pass, it will.

That "supernatural" trust, which is based on revelation and is brought to pass via the power manifestations of healing, miracles, etc, is "the manifestation of faith."

A common pattern involving the manifestation of faith is: God (or the Lord Jesus) gives a revelation, the person trusts the revelation ("the manifestation of faith") and acts on it, and then God supplies the power to bring the revelation to pass.

Moses brought water out of a rock by the manifestation of faith (Exod. 17:5 and 6). He could not do so by his own power, but God told him that if he struck the rock, water would come out.

Moses trusted what God said (the manifestation of faith), acted on it, and by the manifestation of miracles brought water out of the rock. Gideon defeated the Midianites by the manifestation of faith (Judg. 6:16), Elijah multiplied the oil and flour by the manifestation of faith (1 Kings 17:14-16), and the other great miracles of the Bible were done by the manifestation of faith.

When it comes to miracles and gifts of healings, we need the manifestation of faith because we cannot heal the sick or do miracles by our human power.

God must give us a message of knowledge and a message of wisdom, letting us know that it is His will for us to heal someone or do a miracle, and then we must have the faith to do it. As Christians, we should live our lives in such a way that our faith in God grows and continues to grow, so that we are well able to manifest His power and bless and deliver people.

THE POWER OF THE SUPERNATURAL

It does not cost God anything to do a *miracle*. In fact we were told that by the spoken words of God was the heaven created. *God is still operating in the supernatural today. If you are sincere to yourself God will show up suddenly in your life*. Jesus is doing miracles today. I want you to open your eyes and heart to embrace what God is doing especially in your own life.

Do you want to experience the supernatural?

Then you must become dedicated and devoted to the word of God. Humble yourself and see God in everything that you do in life. I see God changing your level. I see God giving you a miracle that you do not deserve.

Chapter 2: Acess Keys to Provoke Divine Intervention

HINDRANCE TO THE SUPERNATURAL

-----Negative mindset---

"And be renewed in the spirit of your mind." Ephesians 4:23

For unless we change the way we think, we will miss the blessing of our prophetic word. If you do not believe in miracles, never expect a miracle to happen in your life.

-------Doubt……

If you doubt miracle. *How can God give you one?* Every time we doubt we make the word of God ineffective in our lives. If you must doubt, doubt yourself. Never doubt God. *"A double minded man is unstable in all his ways."*

THE BLESSINGS OF DIVINE INTERVENTION

--------Continual breakthrough ----------

"But the path of the just is as the shining light, that shineth more and more unto the perfect day." Proverb 4:18

"For thou shalt break forth on the right hand and on the left; and thy seed shall inherit the Gentiles, and make the desolate cities to be inhabited." Isaiah 54:3.

The truth is as long as you keep praying with joy and praise in your lips and heart. Your breakthrough in life is unlimited.

------SUPERNATURAL FAVOR--------

As long as you keep praying in faith, you will continually obtain favor before men

Chapter 2: Acess Keys to Provoke Divine Intervention

and before God. *"And Jesus increased in wisdom and stature, and in favour with God and man."* **Luke 2:52**

"He that diligently seeketh good procureth favour: but he that seeketh mischief, it shall come unto him." **Proverb 11:27.**

Whenever there is favor there is compassion. The bible says "It is of the Lord's mercies that we are not consumed, because his compassions fail not." **Lamentation 3:22**

DIVINE WISDOM

A prayerful man is a man who read his bible. As long as you read your bible you will have access into divine wisdom *"For I will give you a mouth and wisdom, which all your adversaries shall not be able to gainsay nor resist."* **Luke 21:15**

Divine intervention also means Divine wisdom. If you know ahead and see ahead, you will move ahead. Divine wisdom is power, it is stability and progressive. *"But the path of the just is as the shining light, that shineth more and more unto the perfect day."* **Prover4:18**

DAILY STRENGTH

The right word means divine wisdom. It give us courage and boldness to overcome daily obstacles.

CONCLUSION

"And they went forth, and preached every where, the Lord working with them, and confirming the word with signs following. Amen." **Mark16:20**

"…….That confirmeth the word of his servant, and performeth the counsel of his messengers….**Isaiah 44:26**

Chapter 2: Acess Keys to Provoke Divine Intervention

Divine intervention is exclusive for those who understands how the kingdom of God operate. If you are outside of the kingdom of God, I will give you an opportunity to come to Jesus Christ today

"Therefore if any man be in Christ, he is a new creature: old things are passed away; behold, all things are become new". 2cor5:17

I encourage you to repent in prayers of any negative word you have ever spoken against your life and future. Speak the right word and make these confessions boldly in faith.

REPEAT THIS PRAYER AFTER ME....

"Say Lord Jesus, I accept you today, as my Lord and my savior, forgive me of my sins wash me with your blood. Right now, I believe, I am sanctified. I am save. I am free.

The Power of Divine Intervention

I am free from the Power of sin to serve the Lord Jesus. Thank you Lord for saving me. Amen."

What must I do to determine my divine visitation?

To determine divine visitation you must be born again! *The word says as many as received him, to them gave He power to become the sons of God. Even to them that believe on his name.*

To qualify for divine visitation do the following sincerely

1) Acknowledge that you are a sinner and that He died for you.Rom3:23.

2) Repent of your sins. Acts 3:19, Luke13:5, 2Peter3:9

3) Believe in your heart that Jesus died for your sin.Romans10:10

4) Confess Jesus as the Lord over your life. Romans10:10, Acts2:21

Chapter 2: Acess Keys to Provoke Divine Intervention

I really want to hear from you. You can join me if you are in the area to worship with us

MIRACLE OF GOD MINISTRIES INC

343 SANFORD AVENUE NEWARK
NEW JERSEY 07106
Jesus is Lord!

EMAIL: Pastorfranknto@yahoo.com
Website www.fnabaziehealingministries.org

Please feel free to write me

REV FRANKLIN N ABAZIE
33 Schley street Newark
New Jersey 07112

Chapter 2: Acess Keys to Provoke Divine Intervention

WISDOM KEYS

Every Productive Society is a society heading to the top

Millions of Nigerians run away from Nigeria, very few Nigerians stay in Nigeria.

My decision to return Nigeria is the will of God for my life

My short coming in America after 18 years, trained me to be wise, to think, reflect and reason appropriately.

If you train your mind to reason it will train your hands to earn money.

It is absurd to use the money of the heathen to build the kingdom of the living God.

Every Ministry reveals its agenda and goal either at the beginning or at the end. Be careful of your life it is your first Ministry.

The average American mind is conditioned for a continual quest to get new things and (discard the former) and throw away old things.

When I considered well, my BMW jeep became my initial deposit for the work of the ministry in Nigeria

Everyone is waiting for you to change your mind until you change your thinking nothing changes around you.

Multiple academic degrees in other discipline gave me the chance to think, reflect, and reason

What so everyone are thinking and reflecting at the moment reveals you to the time and the now factor

All events and intents are the product of precise thought processes, accurate reason every event is designed for a designated timeline

Chapter 2: Acess Keys to Provoke Divine Intervention

Wisdom is your ability to think, to create and invent. If you can think wise enough you will come out of penury

The distance between you and success is your creative ability to think reason and reflect accurate.

Success is the result of hard work, commitment resolve, and determination, learning from past mistakes and failing.

If you organize your mind you have organized your life and destiny.

There is a thin line between success and failure. If you look above and beyond you are on your way to success.

Wealth is your ability to think, power is your ability to reason and success is your ability to be informed.

If you can make use of your mind by thinking and reasoning God will make use of your life and destiny.

Think and Be Great

Reflect, Reason, think and be great

Famous people are born of woman

That you will make it is your intention; that you will survive is your resolve, that you will succeed with changes is your determination, personal efforts and hard work.

No man was born a failure. Lack of vision is the end product of failure.

Working with mental patients encourages and aspire me to be a productive observant and dedicated to my assignment.

Successful people are not magicians, it is the will power combined with hard work, and determination and a resolve to succeed that make them succeed.

In the unequivocal state of the mind, intention is not a location or a position it is the state of the mind.

Chapter 2: Acess Keys to Provoke Divine Intervention

So many people think that they think. The mind is used to think reflect and reason. You will remain blind with your eye open until you can see with your mind by thinking.

There is no favoritism in accurate and precise calculation

Although knowledge is power, information is the key and gateway to a great future.

It will take the hand of God to move the hand of man.

With the backing of the great wise God, nothing will disconnect you from your inheritance.

As long as you have wisdom and understanding of God, Satan and evil cannot manipulate your life and destiny.

You have come this far by yourself judgment and decision you have made in the past, now lean and listen to God for another dimension of greatness.

Great people are common people it is extra ordinary effort and the price of sacrifice that produces greatness.

As a mental direct care worker I saw a great pastor and a motivational speaker within myself.

Menial job does not reduce your self-worth, until you resolve to achieve greatness see greatness in all you do; you will never count in your community.

The principle of Jesus will solve your gambling and addiction problems

The man of Jesus will lead you into heaven,

Everyone have their self-appraisal and what they think about you. Until you discover yourself other opinion about you will alter the real you.

Supervisors and directors are just a position in the chain of command in a work place.

Chapter 2: Acess Keys to Provoke Divine Intervention

Never allow your supervisor hierarchy to alter your opinion about yourself.

Everyone can come out of debt if they make up their mind.

That I am not a decision maker at work does not diminish my contribution to my world.

Although it appears like it was a poor decision to accept a direct care employment at a psychiatric hospital as I reflect of my nine years of experience, it became apparent that I have learnt and experienced enough for my next assignment.

Self-encouragement and determination is a resolve of the heart.

If you are determined to make a difference, and do the things that make a difference you will eventually make a difference.

Good things do not come easy

Short cuts will cut your life short.

The Power of Divine Intervention

Those who look ahead move ahead.

Life is all about making an impact. In your life time strive to make an impact in your community.

Make friends and connect with people who are moving ahead of you in life.

If you can look around well you have come a long way in your life, made a lot of difference and realized a lot of success in life.

If you are my old friend, hurry up to reach out to me before I become a stranger to you.

Everything I am blessed with inspirations from God, that change my definition and interpretation of the world around me.

I thought I was stagnant and lonely until I looked around and noticed my children running around and my wife cooking.

Chapter 2: Acess Keys to Provoke Divine Intervention

At 40 I resigned my Job to seek the Lord forever.

My ministry took a drastic rise to the top when the wisdom of God visited me with knowledge and understanding.

You will be a better person if you understand the characteristics of your personality – your mood swings attitudes and habits.

It is the seed of love you sow into the heart of a child and a woman that you reap in due time.

Love is not selfish, love share everything including the concealed secrets of the mind.

As long as you have a prayer life and a bible; you will never feel lonely, rejected, and idle in the race of life.

When good friends disconnect from you, let them go, they might have seen something new in a different direction.

Confidence in yourself and in God is the only way to bring you out of captivity

Never train a child to waste his/her time.

The mind is the greatest assets of a great future.

You walk by common sense run by principles and fly by instruction.

PRAYER POINTS AGAINST CORONAVIRUS

"While men slept, his enemy came and sowed tares among the wheat, and went his way." (Matthew 13:25)

Coronavirus came suddenly, we will prayer against it suddenly.

1. My Father, I am in your hand, avenge me of my adversaries, in Jesus Name.

2. Coronavirus witchcraft, I destroy your nets in the Name of Jesus

Chapter 2: Acess Keys to Provoke Divine Intervention

3. My stubborn enemies, I drag you to the court of the Almighty, in Jesus Name.

4. Enemies of my progress, I drag you to the court of the Almighty, in Jesus Name.

5. God Arise! Judge them by fire! in Jesus Name.

6. Garment of darkness on my body, CATCH FIRE! in Jesus Name.

7. Power of environmental covens, Die, in Jesus Name.

8. Opportunity wasters, my life is not your candidate, Die! in Jesus Name.

9. Any chain binding my finances, Break Now! in Jesus Name.

10. Spiritual powerlessness, Die! in Jesus Name.

The Power of Divine Intervention

11. Drinkers of blood and eaters of flesh, Hear the word of the Lord, DIE! in Jesus Name.

12. My inner-man RECEIVE FIRE! (Pray it like machine-gun by repeating it several times), in Jesus Name.

13. By the power that healed blind Bartemaeus, O God Arise! Heal me by Fire! in Jesus Name.

14. Power of infirmity, Die, in Jesus Name.

15. Inherited infirmities, you are a liar! Die! in Jesus Name.

16. Blood of Jesus, sanitize my blood, in Jesus Name.

17. Witchcraft-sponsored infirmities, BACK-FIRE! in Jesus Name.

18. Bondage of infirmities, B-R-E-A-K! in Jesus Name.

Chapter 2: Acess Keys to Provoke Divine Intervention

19. Curses of infirmity B-R-E-A-K! in Jesus Name.

20. Any power prolonging infirmity, DIE! in Jesus Name.

21. Eaters of flesh; Drinkers of blood, my life is not your candidate, therefore, DIE! in Jesus Name.

22. Arrows of infirmity assigned against my head, B-A-C-K-F-I-R-E! in Jesus Name.

23. Agents of infirmity from my food, Die! in Jesus Name.

24. My Father, You are the One who created times and seasons, and You put me here to operate, I thank You Father for bringing me here today, by the power of the Holy Ghost, I recover my destiny from the hands of the wicked. Father, as David cried unto You, so do I cry today, that:

Father, my times are in Your Hands deliver me from my wicked enemies. OH GOD ARISE AND RESCUE MY DESTINY FROM THE HANDS OF THE WICKED in Jesus Name.

25. I come against the spirit of coronavirus in the name of Jesus.

26. Every altar of darkness raised against me in the heavenlies, DIE! in Jesus Name. (Kill the altar of darkness).

27. Every problem programmed into my life from the heavenlies, DIE! in Jesus Name.

28. Blood of Jesus, Wipe Out, the handwriting of darkness assigned against me in the heavenlies, in Jesus Name.

29. Every arrow fired against me from the heavenlies, B-A-C-K-F-I-R-E! in Jesus Name.

Chapter 2: Acess Keys to Provoke Divine Intervention

30. Every diviner assigned against me from the heavenlies, RUN MAD! in Jesus Name.

31. My Father! Arise! Fight for me Now! in Jesus Name.

32. Every power assigned to destroy my destiny, DIE! in Jesus Name.

33. Every power of frustration that pursued me last year, Your Time Is Up! DIE! in Jesus Name.

34. Every enemy of my promotion and advancement S-C-A-T-T-E-R in Jesus Name.

35. Every operation of darkness in my family line, DIE! in Jesus Name.

36. I shall have unstoppable advancement in Jesus Name.

37. This year, the wealth of the unbelievers shall be transferred to my bosom, in Jesus Name.

The Power of Divine Intervention

38. This year, my star shall arise and fall no more, in Jesus Name.

39. This year, men shall chase me around with blessings, in Jesus Name.

40. I recover ten-fold all my wasted years, in Jesus Name.

41. Every power of the night programmed against my progress, S-C-A-T-T-E-R! in Jesus Name.

42. Mountain of affliction before me, S-C-A-T-T-E-R! in Jesus Name.

43. Every dream affliction, Die! in Jesus Name.

44. This year, men shall compete to favour me, in Jesus Name.

45. Every evil hand that shall point to my star this year, W-H-I-T-H-E-R! in Jesus Name.

Chapter 2: Acess Keys to Provoke Divine Intervention

46. Every satanic malpractice over my family, I cut you off! in Jesus Name.

47. Every power assigned to use my life as a dumping ground, C-A-T-C-H-F-I-R-E! in Jesus Name.

48. Every tree of failure of my father's house, Die! in Jesus Name.

49. (Sing three hot songs with boiling aggression… No. 1 song: Let God Arise and my enemies be scattered [3ce] Let God, My God Arise. No. 2 song: The Lion of Judah has broken every yoke, He has given me the victory again and again. No. 3 song:

    The walls of Jericho fell down flat, As children of God we're praising the Lord, the walls of Jericho fell down flat.) EVERY

    WALL OF JERICHO ASSIGNED AGAINST MY SUCCESS, S-C-A-T-T-E-R! in Jesus Name.

50. Every opposition against my possession, DIE! in Jesus Name.

51. Every tongue anointed by satan to speak against my life, You Are A LIAR! DIE! in Jesus Name.

52. Every power declaring that it is over for me, You Are A LIAR! DIE! in Jesus Name.

53. Every good thing that I have laid my hands upon, my hands shall finish it, in Jesus Name.

54. Every yoke upon my hands, B-R-E-A-K! in Jesus Name.

55. Any curse issued against my hands, B-R-E-A-K! in Jesus Name.

56. Thou power of poor finishing, DIE! in Jesus Name. (I refuse to finish poor).

57. Thou power of bad luck, DIE! in Jesus Name.

Chapter 2: Acess Keys to Provoke Divine Intervention

58. Serpents of death; serpents of wastage, assigned against my hands, DIE! in Jesus Name.

59. Every strongman assigned against my hands, What Are You Waiting For? DIE! in Jesus Name.

60. Every evil power of my father's house assigned against my hands, DIE! in Jesus Name. (Lift up your two hands and wave it to the Lord, as u are waving those hands, every arrow of darkness upon the hands is being shaken out, every cobwebs and spirit of death and hell upon the hand are being taken out....)

61. Blood of Jesus, Arise in your POWER! ENVELOPE my hands! in Jesus Name. (declare this seven times with faith in your voice: "My hands have laid foundations, my hands shall also finish it in the name of Jesus").

62. My hands shall bury bad things; it shall not bury good things, in Jesus Name.

63. Any power that has tied down my destiny, BREAK-LOOSE, from my life, in Jesus Name.

64. Wherever the stars have been programmed to disturb my destiny, O God Arise! Manifest your POWER! in Jesus Name.

65. Every witchcraft power toying with my destiny, DIE! in Jesus Name.

66. God of Elijah! ATTACK my red sea! in Jesus Name.

67. My Father! Reshuffle my environment to favour me! in Jesus Name. (Let there be a re-shuflement to favour me).

68. My Father! If I have been disconnected from the socket of my

Chapter 2: Acess Keys to Provoke Divine Intervention

destiny, reconnect me by fire! in Jesus Name.

69. My Father, whatever you have not positioned into my life, wipe them off! in Jesus Name.

70. God Arise! And dismantle the poison in my foundation! in Jesus Name.

71. Negative circumstances that is affecting my success, BOW! in Jesus Name.

72. I curse the spirit of backwardness, in Jesus Name.

73. Every witchcraft register bearing my destiny, C-A-T-C-H-F-I-R-E! in Jesus Name.

74. Every power delaying the manifestation of my breakthroughs, DIE! in Jesus Name.

The Power of Divine Intervention

75. God Arise! And rearrange my circumstances to bring me into glory! in Jesus Name.

76. Every proclamation of the powers of darkness against my life, DIE! in Jesus Name.

77. God Arise! And package testimonies for me in Jesus Name.

78. Satanic decree working against my life, DIE! in Jesus Name. (Nullify the decree, cancel it).

79. Every calendar of the enemy, working against my life, CLEAR AWAY! in Jesus Name.

80. You evil programmers, let me go! in Jesus Name.

81. Anything programmed into my foundation to waste my destiny, DIE! in Jesus Name.

Chapter 2: Acess Keys to Provoke Divine Intervention

82. Any seasonal problem, programmed into my life, I de-programme you by fire! in Jesus Name.

83. You altar of evil programmers, assigned against my life, DIE! in Jesus Name.

84. My Father! If I have obeyed any evil command, KILL IT! in the name of Jesus.

85. Witchcraft programming; You are A LIAR! DIE! in the name of Jesus.

86. Any negative power, programmed against my head, JUMP OUT NOW! in the name of Jesus.

87. Satanic programming in the dream, Your Time Is Up! Therefore, DIE! in the name of Jesus.

88. Every witchcraft material planted into my life from the womb, DIE! in the name of Jesus.

The Power of Divine Intervention

89. In the Name of the King of kings, In the name of the Lord of lords, In the name of the President of presidents: JESUS CHRIST! Every witchcraft bondage in my life, B-R-E-A-K!

90. Any power calling my name into a cauldron, You Are A LIAR! DIE! in the name of Jesus.

91. Blood of Jesus, WIPE OFF every witchcraft name assigned against me, in the name of Jesus.

92. Every witchcraft padlock assigned against me, LOCK UP YOUR OWNER, in the name of Jesus.

93. Every astral projection against my life, BE ARRESTED! in the name of Jesus.

94. Every witchcraft power that have set eyes on me, RECEIVE BLINDNESS! in the name of Jesus.

Chapter 2: Acess Keys to Provoke Divine Intervention

95. Every witchcraft coven assigned against my destiny, S-C-A-T-T-E-R! in the name of Jesus.

96. Poverty stronghold, I cast u down, I set u ablaze! in the name of Jesus.

97. Every power contesting for my oil, DIE! in the name of Jesus.

98. Every good thing stolen from my life by night, COME BACK NOW! in the name of Jesus.

99. Every good thing stolen from my life by the day, COME BACK! in the name of Jesus.

100. Arrows of the day, Arrows of the night assigned against my life, B-A-C-K-F-I-R-E! in the name of Jesus.

101. Every mouth of the wicked speaking against me, SHUT UP! in the name of Jesus.

The Power of Divine Intervention

102. Ministry of fear in my life, DIE! DIE!! DIE!!! in the name of Jesus.

103. Every power stealing my promotion, DIE! in the name of Jesus.

104. Every abnormal pattern in my family line, DIE! in the name of Jesus. [Pray this seven hot times]

105. God Arise and make me a wonder! in the name of Jesus.

106. Every power reporting me to witchcraft meetings, DIE! DIE!! DIE!!! in the name of Jesus.

107. Every meeting summoned to waste my life, in the name of Jesus.

108. Information about my life present on any wicked altar, C-A-T-C-H-F-I-R-E! in the name of Jesus.

109. Camera of darkness, taking my pictures in the dark world, C-A-T-C-H-F-I-R-E! in the name of Jesus.

Chapter 2: Acess Keys to Provoke Divine Intervention

110. Every inherited power assigned to waste my destiny, COME OUT NOW! In the name of Jesus.

111. Communication gadgets of darkness transferring my information, C-A-T-C-H-F-I-R-E! in the name of Jesus.

112. Every agenda of coronavirus against our life, DIE! in the name of Jesus.

113. My wealth, buried in the earth, COME FORTH! in the name of Jesus.

114. Every arrow of witchcraft fired into my prosperity, DIE!!! in the name of Jesus.

115. Garment of poverty, C-A-T-C-H-F-I-R-E! in the name of Jesus.

116. You financial killer of my father's house, I am not your candidate! Therefore, DIE!!! in the name of Jesus.

117. Expected and unexpected financial breakthrough, LOCATE ME BY FIRE! in the name of Jesus.

118. Poverty activator dreams, Hear the word of the Lord! S-C-A-T-T-E-R! in the name of Jesus.

119. God Arise and use me to change my family history, in the name of Jesus.

120. My end shall be better than my beginning, in the name of Jesus.

121. Anything buried that is pulling me down, DIE! in the name of Jesus.

122. Oracles of my father's house, speaking against my progress, in the name of Jesus.

123. Power of collective captivity, my life is not your candidate, therefore, S-C-A-T-T-E-R! in the name of Jesus.

Chapter 2: Acess Keys to Provoke Divine Intervention

124. Parental curses that is working against my life CLEAR AWAY!!! in the name of Jesus.

125. I re-write my family history by the power in the blood of Jesus.

126. Any problem that came into my life through any dead relative, you are a liar, DIE!!! in the name of Jesus.

127. My life, reject wastage, in the name of Jesus.

128. Every agenda of the enemy to capture my spirit-man, FAIL! in the name of Jesus.

129. Spirit of perdition, spirit of perverseness, LOOSE YOUR HOLD, upon my life, in the name of Jesus.

130. Every power tying me down to iniquity, B-R-E-A-K-A-W-A-Y!!! in the name of Jesus.

The Power of Divine Intervention

131. Hell fire shall not harvest my life, in the name of Jesus.

132. My Father, if I am presently wrongly scheduled, RESCHEDULE ME! in the name of Jesus.

133. The enemy would not write the last chapter of my life, in the name of Jesus.

134. Every evil master, rejoicing at my sadness, DIE! in the name of Jesus.

135. Every power drawing my virtues, You are a LIAR! DIE! in the name of Jesus.

136. My transferred blessings, hear the word of the Lord, C-O-M-E B-A-C-K!!! in the name of Jesus.

137. Every padlock holding down my progress, C-A-T-C-H-F-I-R-E! in the name of Jesus.

Chapter 2: Acess Keys to Provoke Divine Intervention

138. Spiritual robbers in my habitation, LOOSE YOUR POWER!!! in the name of Jesus.

139. I roast by Fire! The Spirit of fear against coronavirus in the name of Jesus.

140. Power of hardship, DIE!!! in the name of Jesus.

141. Merchants of souls, assigned against my destiny, DIE! in the name of Jesus.

142. My heavens OPEN! My rain of blessing FALL!! in the name of Jesus.

143. My Father, do anything to turn my life around, in the name of Jesus.

144. Commanded blessings! Overtaking Blessings!! Added Blessings!!! APPEAR IN MY LIFE!!! in the name of Jesus.

The Power of Divine Intervention

145. God of the turn-around, I am here, LOCATE ME NOW! in the name of Jesus.

146. Star Hunters, assigned against me, DIE! in the name of Jesus.

147. Powers assigned to make my life useless, DIE! in the name of Jesus.

148. My breakthroughs from the 4 corners of the earth, LOCATE ME NOW! in the name of Jesus.

149. Any power disconnecting me from the virtues of the Lord, DIE! in the name of Jesus.

150. My lost FIRE! COME BACK!!! in the name of Jesus.

151. Powers assigned to push me to the back, E-X-P-I-R-E!!! in the name of Jesus.

152. In my dream life, My Father, APPEAR!!! in the name of Jesus.

Chapter 2: Acess Keys to Provoke Divine Intervention

153. My eyes OPEN! SEE the Lord!! in the name of Jesus.

154. What stopped my father, will not stop me! in the name of Jesus.

155. Power of limitation, you are a LIAR! DIE!!! in the name of Jesus.

156. I dismantle every power of backwardness, in the name of Jesus.

157. Every power assigned to disorganise my life, you are a LIAR! DIE! in the name of Jesus.

158. My hands Receive power to prosper, in the name of Jesus.

159. My Father, rearrange my circumstances to catapult my life, in the name of Jesus.

160. I come against sickness and disease in this coronavirus pandemic in Jesus Mighty Name. AMEN

CHAPTER 3

PRAYER OF SALVATION

> "Neither is there salvation in any other: for there is none other name under heaven given among men, whereby we must be saved."
>
> **Acts4:12**

And so all Israel shall be saved: as it is written, There shall come out of Sion the Deliverer, and shall turn away ungodliness from Jacob:

Romans11:26

What must I do to determine my salvation?

To be saved we must be born again! The word says as many as received him, to them gave He power to become the sons of God. Even to them that believe on his name.

Chapter 3 : Prayer of Salvation

To qualify for divine visitation do the following sincerely

1) Acknowledge that you are a sinner and that He died for you.Rom3:23.

2) Repent of your sins. Acts 3:19, Luke13:5, 2Peter3:9

3) Believe in your heart that Jesus died for your sin.Romans10:10

4) Confess Jesus as the Lord over your life. Romans10:10, Acts2:21

Are you saved?

If God have saved your life, speak to someone about Jesus. Disciple someone to join you worship the Lord Jesus Christ.

MIRACLE CARE OUTREACH

"...But that the members should have the same care one for another" 1cor12:25

We are all members of the body of Christ. Jesus commanded us to love our neighbor as ourselves. This includes caring for one another as a member of one body. True love is expressed in caring and giving. The word says for God so Love He gave....

Reach out to someone in need of Jesus, help someone in crisis find Christ. Look out and prove your love to Jesus by caring and inviting your friends and associates to find Jesus the Healer.

Invite your friends to our Home Care Cell Fellowship (Miracle chapel Intl Satellite fellowship) In the USA at 33 Schley Street Newark New Jersey 07112.

If you are in Nigeria—**MIRACLE OF GOD MINISTRIES**

Chapter 3 : Prayer of Salvation

A.K.A **"MIRACLE CHAPEL INTL"** Mpama –Egbu-Owerri Imo state Nigeria.

(Home Care Cell fellowship Group). We meet every Tuesday at 6:00pm-7:00pm.

LIFE IS NOT ALL ABOUT DURATION BUT ITS ALL ABOUT DONATION

What does the above statement mean?

Life consists not in accumulation of material wealth. (Luke12:15) But it's all about liberality….meaning- what you can give and share with others. Proverb11:25. When you live for others--You live forever- because you out live your generation by the legacy you live behind after you depart into glory to be with the Lord. But when you live to yourself - you are reduced to self—you are easily forgotten when you die and depart in glory. Permit me to admonish you today to live your life to be a blessing to a soul connected to you today. I want you to know that so many souls are connected and looking up to you, and through you so many souls will be saved and rescued from destruction. Will you disciple someone today to find Jesus Christ?

As a genuine Christian; it is your duty to evangelize Jesus Christ to all you meet on your way. Jesus is still in the healing business-Jesus is still doing miracles from time of old to now. Therefore tell someone about Jesus Christ today, disciple and bring them to Church. John 1:45 *Philip findeth Nathanael....*

Please to prove the sincerity of your love for God today; please become a soul winner. The dignity of your Christianity is hidden in your boldness to proclaim and evangelize Jesus Christ to all you meet on your way. There is a question mark on the integrity of your Christianity until you become a life soul winner. Invite someone to join us worship the Lord Jesus this coming Sunday. Amen

Chapter 3 : Prayer of Salvation

MIRACLE OF GOD MINISTRIES PILLARS OF THE COMMISSION

We Believe Preach and Practice the following

1) We believe and preach Salvation to every living human being

2) We believe and preach Repentance and forgiveness of sins

3) We believe and preach the baptism of the Holy Spirit and Spiritual gifts

4) We believe and teach the Prosperity

5) We believe and preach Divine Healing and Miracles (Signs &Wonder)

6) We believe and preach Faith

7) We believe and proclaim the Power of God (Supernatural)

8) We believe and proclaim Praise& Worship to God

9) We believe and preach Wisdom

10) We believe and preach Holiness (Consecration)

11) We believe and preach Vision

12) We believe and teach the Word of God

13) We believe and teach Success

14) We believe and practice Prayer

15) We believe and teach Deliverance

This 15 stones form the Pillars of Our Commission. Become part of this church family and follow this great move of God.

MY HEART FELT PRAYER FOR YOU

It is my prayer for timely divine intervention upon your life. May all prevailing circumstances against your life lose its stronghold in Jesus Name.

Chapter 3 : Prayer of Salvation

Now let me Pray for you:

It is written

"For the earnest expectation of the creature waiteth for the manifestation of the sons of God.." **Romans8:19**

But as many as received him, to them gave he power to become the sons of God, even to them that believe on his name

THE POWER OF EVANGELISM

"Go ye therefore, and teach all nations, baptizing them in the name of the Father, and of the Son, and of the Holy Ghost:" **Mathew28:19**

Evangelism has power to attract the blessing of the Lord upon our lives. It is written "And ye shall serve the Lord your God, and he shall bless thy bread, and thy water; and I will take sickness away from the midst of thee." Exodus23:26.

Evangelizing, and bringing men and women to the cross of Jesus Christ is a great commandment. According to the above scripture, we are commanded to teach all nations, the name of Jesus Christ.

It is my prayer that you will witness the name of Jesus Christ to someone today.

Remember..........

"And they that be wise shall shine as the brightness of the firmament; and they that turn many to righteousness as the stars for ever and ever." **Daniel12:3**

OPERATION--"ONE MAN TEN MEN"

"Thus saith the Lord of hosts; In those days it shall come to pass, that ten men shall take hold out of all languages of the nations, even shall take hold of the skirt of him that is a Jew, saying, We will go with you:

Chapter 3 : Prayer of Salvation

for we have heard that God is with you."
Zachariah 8:23

If someone directed you to this ministry, it is divine wisdom for you to bring someone else also. If you googled to come into contact with us, I will recommend you also tell ten of your contacts and share with them what Jesus is doing through this ministry. Tell everybody about Jesus, also tell them to contact this ministry. Jesus is Lord!!

OPERATION ONE MAN ONE SOUL

If you cannot bring ten people at one time, at least you can talk to one person per time.

I recommend that you look for just one person who will respond positively and bring them to church. Or tell them about this ministry. That convert, is your own convert minister to them the love of Jesus Christ.

JESUS IS LORD!

CHAPTER 4
ABOUT THE AUTHOR

Rev Franklin N Abazie is the founding and Presiding Pastor of Miracle of God Ministries with headquarters in Newark, New Jersey USA and a branch church in Owerri- Imo State Nigeria. He is following the footsteps of one of his mentors, Oral Roberts (Healing Evangelist) of the blessed memory. The Lord passed Oral Roberts healing mantle two days before he went to be with the Lord at age 91 into the hand of healing evangelist-Rev Franklin N Abazie in a vision.

In all his services the Power and Presence of God is present to heal all in his audience. He is an ordained man of God with a Healing Ministry reviving the healing and miracle ministry of Jesus Christ of Nazareth.

Chapter 4 : About The Author

Pastor Franklin N Abazie, is called by God with a unique mandate: **"THE MOMENT IS DUE TO IMPACT YOUR WORLD THROUGH THE REVIVAL OF THE HEALING & MIRACLE MINISTRY OF JESUS CHRIST OF NAZARETH**

I AM SENDING YOU TO RESTORE HEALTH UNTO THEE AND I WILL HEAL THEE OF THY WOUNDS. SAID THE LORD OF HOST"

He is a gifted ardent Teacher of the word of God who operates also in the office of a Prophet, generating and attracting undeniable signs & wonders, special miracles and healings, with apostolic fireworks of the Holy Ghost. He is the founding and presiding senior Pastor of this fast growing Healing ministry. He has written over 86 inspirational, healing and transforming books covering almost all aspect of divine healing and life. He is happily married and blessed with children.

Chapter 4 : About The Author

BOOKS BY REV FRANKLIN N ABAZIE

1) Commanding Abundance
2) The outcome of faith
3) Understanding the secret of prevailing prayers.
4) Understanding the secret of the man God uses
5) Activating my due Season
6) Overcoming Divine Verdicts
7) The Outcome of Divine Wisdom
8) Understanding God's Restoration Mandate
9) Walking in the Victory and Authority of the truth
10) Gods Covenant Exemption
11) Destiny Restoration Pillars

12) Provoking Acceptable Praise
13) Understanding Divine Judgment
14) Activating Angelic Re-enforcement
15) Provoking Un-Merited Favor
16) The Benefits of the Speaking faith
17) Understanding Divine Arrangement
18) Understanding Divine Healing
19) The Mystery of Endurance
20) Obeying Divine Instructions
21) Understanding the Voice of God
22) Never give up on Hope
23) The prevailing Power of faith
24) Understanding Divine Prosperity
25) The Reward of Prayer
26) Covenant Keys to Answered Prayers
27) Activating the Forces of Vengeance

Chapter 4 : About The Author

28) Put your faith to work
29) Where is your trust?
30) The Audacity of the Blood of Jesus
31) Redeeming Your Days
32) The Force of Vision
33) Breaking the shackles of Family curses
34) Wisdom for Marriage Stability
35) Overcoming prevailing challenges
36) The Prayer solution
39) The power of Prayer
40) Prayer strategy
41) The prayer that works
42) Walking in Forgiveness
43) The Power of the grace of God
44) The Power of Persistence
45) The benefit of the speaking faith.

46) Fearless faith
47) Redeeming Your Days.
48) The Supernatural Power of Prophecy
49) The companionship of the Holy Spirit
50) Understanding Divine Judgement
51) Understanding Divine Prosperity
52) Dominating Controlling Forces
53) The winner's Faith
54) Destiny Restoration Pillars
55) Developing Spiritual Muscles
56) Inexplicable faith
57) The lifestyle of Prayer
58) Developing a positive attitude in life.
59) The Mystery of Divine supply
60) Encounter with the Power of God
61) Walking in love

Chapter 4 : About The Author

62) Praying in the Spirit
63) How to provoke your testimony
64) Walking in the reality of the anointing
65) The Reality of new birth
66) The Price of freedom
67) The Supernatural Power of faith
68) The intellectual components of Redemption.
69) Overcoming Fear
70) Overcoming Prevailing Challenges
71) My life & Ministry
72) The Mystery of Praise
73) Commanding faith
74) The Power of bold Declaration
75) The Power of Divine Intervention
76) Dream Big & Believe in your self

MIRACLE OF GOD MINISTRIES

*NIGERIA CRUSADE
2012*

MIRACLE OF GOD MINISTRIES

NIGERIA CRUSADE 2012

MIRACLE OF GOD MINISTRIES

NIGERIA CRUSADE
2012

www.ingramcontent.com/pod-product-compliance
Lightning Source LLC
Chambersburg PA
CBHW030332100526
44592CB00010B/672